An Introduction to The Gene Keys:

A Beginners Guide To Better Understanding Yourself.

Jenna Parker

Table of Contents

An Introduction to The Gene Keys: 1
   A Beginners Guide To Better Understanding Yourself. 1

Introduction 5
   Throughout this book, you'll discover: 5

Chapter 1: Understanding Gene Keys 7
   Summary 11

Chapter 2: The Three Sequences 13
   The Activation Sequence 13
   The Venus Sequence 16
   The Pearl Sequence 19
   Summary 21

Chapter 3: The Benefits of Gene Keys Readings 23
   Personal Growth and Transformation 23
   Deepening Self-Awareness and Self-Compassion 26
   Enhancing Relationships and Communication 26
   Spiritual Growth and Enlightenment 27
   Summary 30

Chapter 4: Interpreting Your Hologenetic Profile 31
   Obtaining Your Hologenetic Profile 31
   Interpreting Your Profile 34
   Putting It All Together 37
   Practical Examples and Techniques 37
   Summary 39

Chapter 5: Practical Applications of Gene Keys 41
   Self-Discovery and Personal Development 41
   Spiritual Evolution and Enlightenment 42
   Exercises and Techniques 47
   Summary 53

Chapter 6: Common Misunderstandings of Gene Keys 54
   Misunderstanding 1: Gene Keys are deterministic or fatalistic 54
   Misunderstanding 2: Shadows are negative traits to be eliminated 55
   Misunderstanding 3: Gene Keys are only about individual growth 56
   Guidance for navigating misunderstandings 56
   Summary 58

Chapter 7: Case Studies and Examples 59
   Case Study 1: Sarah's Journey of Self-Discovery 59
   Case Study 2: Michael's Path of Spiritual Awakening 61

    Case Study 3: Lisa's Journey of Embodiment 62
    Summary 63

Chapter 8: Resources and Further Reading *64*
    Books by Richard Rudd 64
    Online Courses and Programs 65
    Online Communities and Forums 66
    Retreats and Live Events 67
    Some of the most popular Gene Keys events include: 67
    Conclusion 68

Appendices *70*
    Appendix A: Glossary of Gene Keys Terminology 70
    Appendix B: Worksheets and Reflection Questions 71
    Appendix C: Additional Resources and Recommendations 73

Jenna Parker

Introduction

Welcome to "An Introduction to The Gene Keys: A Beginners Guide To Better Understanding Yourself." If you're new to the concept of Gene Keys and are curious about how they can help you unlock your potential, gain self-awareness, and embark on a journey of personal growth, you've come to the right place.

Gene Keys is a fascinating and transformative tool that combines the wisdom of ancient spiritual traditions with modern genetic science. It offers a unique perspective on understanding yourself, your relationships, and your place in the world. However, for many beginners, the concept of Gene Keys can seem daunting or esoteric at first glance.

That's where this book comes in. Our goal is to demystify Gene Keys and provide you with a clear, accessible, and comprehensive introduction to this powerful system. We'll guide you step by step through the basics of Gene Keys, explaining key concepts in simple terms and providing practical examples and applications.

Throughout this book, you'll discover:

1. The origins and philosophy behind Gene Keys
2. The three main sequences: Activation Sequence, Venus Sequence, and Pearl Sequence
3. The benefits of Gene Keys readings for personal growth and self-discovery
4. How to interpret your own Hologenetic Profile
5. Practical ways to apply Gene Keys in your daily life
6. Common misunderstandings and how to overcome them

7. Real-life case studies and examples of transformation through Gene Keys
8. Resources and recommendations for further exploration

Whether you're seeking to overcome personal challenges, improve your relationships, or simply gain a deeper understanding of yourself, Gene Keys offers a rich and rewarding path. By the end of this book, you'll have a solid foundation in the principles and applications of Gene Keys, empowering you to embark on your own journey of self-discovery and transformation.

So, let's dive in and unlock the power of Gene Keys together. Get ready to explore a new way of understanding yourself and the world around you, and to discover the incredible potential that lies within.

Chapter 1: Understanding Gene Keys

Welcome to the fascinating world of Gene Keys!

In this chapter, we'll explore the origins and background of this transformative system, define key terms, and delve into the philosophy and principles that form the foundation of Gene Keys.

Origins and Background

Gene Keys is a groundbreaking system that bridges the gap between ancient wisdom traditions and modern scientific understanding, offering a unique and profound approach to personal growth and transformation. The creator of Gene Keys, Richard Rudd, embarked on a remarkable journey of exploration and synthesis that led to the birth of this powerful tool for self-discovery and spiritual awakening.

Rudd's journey began with an in-depth study of the I Ching, an ancient Chinese divination text that has served as a wellspring of wisdom and insight for countless generations. The I Ching, with its 64 hexagrams, has influenced and inspired spiritual and philosophical traditions across the world, offering a timeless framework for understanding the nature of reality and the human experience.

Alongside his exploration of the I Ching, Rudd immersed himself in the study of Kabbalah, a mystical branch of Judaism that delves into the esoteric aspects of creation and the divine. Kabbalah's intricate system of symbols, archetypes, and teachings provided Rudd with a rich tapestry of wisdom and a deeper understanding of the interconnectedness of all things.

Rudd also found inspiration in the teachings of Sri Aurobindo, an Indian philosopher, yogi, and spiritual reformer. Sri Aurobindo's integral approach to spirituality, which sought to harmonize the ancient wisdom of the East with the scientific understanding of the West, resonated deeply with Rudd's own vision of a holistic and integrative path to transformation.

As Rudd delved deeper into these ancient wisdom traditions, he began to discern a common thread that wove them together — a profound understanding of human consciousness and its vast potential for growth and transformation. This realization sparked a profound curiosity in Rudd, leading him to explore the emerging field of genetics and the discovery of the 64 codons within human DNA.

The 64 codons, which form the basis of the genetic code, are the building blocks of all life on Earth. Rudd intuited a deep connection between these fundamental units of biology and the timeless wisdom of the I Ching and other spiritual traditions. He recognized that the 64 codons could serve as a powerful symbolic language for mapping the 64 archetypes of human consciousness and potential.

In a moment of profound insight and revelation, Rudd received a transmission of the 64 Gene Keys — a system that elegantly maps each of the 64 codons to a specific aspect of human consciousness and potential. This transmission, which came to Rudd as a fully-formed vision, laid the foundation for the Gene Keys teachings that have since transformed the lives of countless individuals around the world.

Through his tireless work and dedication, Rudd has developed and refined the Gene Keys system, creating a comprehensive framework for self-discovery and transformation that draws upon the deep wisdom of ancient traditions while remaining grounded in the cutting-edge insights of modern science. By sharing the Gene Keys teachings with others, Rudd has empowered thousands of individuals to unlock their unique gifts, overcome their challenges, and embark upon a profound journey of personal and spiritual growth.

The origins and background of Gene Keys serve as a testament to the power of synthesis and the enduring wisdom of ancient spiritual traditions. By bridging the gap between these timeless teachings and the frontiers of modern scientific understanding, Richard Rudd has created a truly revolutionary tool for self-discovery and transformation that has the potential to catalyze a profound shift in human consciousness and awakening.

Key Terms

To understand Gene Keys, it's essential to familiarize yourself with a few key terms:

1. Gene Keys: The 64 Gene Keys represent specific facets of human consciousness and potential. Each Gene Key is associated with a shadow, a gift, and a siddhi (a higher state of consciousness).

2. Hologenetic Profile: Your Hologenetic Profile is a unique map of your personal Gene Keys, based on your date, time, and place of birth. It reveals your innate strengths, challenges, and opportunities for growth.

3. Activation Sequence: The Activation Sequence is one of the three main sequences in Gene Keys. It represents your life's journey, from your birth to your ultimate realization, and is divided into three stages: the Shadow, the Gift, and the Siddhi.

Philosophy and Principles

At its core, Gene Keys is a path of self-discovery and transformation. It is based on the principle that within each of us lies a vast potential waiting to be unlocked. By understanding and embracing our shadows—the limiting patterns and beliefs that hold us back—we can transform them into gifts and, ultimately, siddhis.

Gene Keys teaches that our challenges and struggles are not obstacles to be overcome but opportunities for growth and evolution. By facing our shadows with compassion and awareness, we can tap into the hidden gifts within us and realize our highest potential.

Another key principle of Gene Keys is the interconnectedness of all things. Just as the 64 codons in our DNA are intimately connected, so too are we connected to each other and to the greater web of life. By understanding our place in this larger tapestry, we can cultivate a sense of purpose, meaning, and belonging.

Gene Keys also emphasizes the power of contemplation and self-reflection. Rather than offering a prescriptive path, it invites us to explore our own inner landscape and discover our unique truth. Through practices such as meditation, journaling, and deep listening, we can cultivate a profound relationship with ourselves and access the wisdom that lies within.

Ultimately, Gene Keys is a path of liberation—from our limiting patterns, from our suffering, and from the illusion of separation. By embracing our shadows, cultivating our gifts, and realizing our siddhis, we can awaken to our true nature and live a life of authenticity, purpose, and joy.

Summary

In this chapter, we've explored the origins and background of Gene Keys, defined key terms, and delved into the philosophy and principles that form its foundation. As you continue your journey with Gene Keys, remember that this is a path of self-discovery and transformation. Trust in the wisdom that lies within you, and allow the Gene Keys to guide you on your unique path of unfolding.

In the next chapter, we'll dive deeper into the three main sequences of Gene Keys—the Activation Sequence, the Venus Sequence, and the Pearl Sequence—and explore how they can support you on your journey of personal growth and transformation.

Jenna Parker

Chapter 2: The Three Sequences

In the world of Gene Keys, there are three main sequences that form the backbone of this transformative system: the Activation Sequence, the Venus Sequence, and the Pearl Sequence. Each sequence represents a unique path of personal growth and evolution, focusing on different aspects of our lives and consciousness.

In this chapter, we'll dive deeper into each of these sequences and explore how they can support you on your journey of self-discovery and transformation.

The Activation Sequence

The Activation Sequence is the cornerstone of the Gene Keys system, providing a profound and illuminating map of your life's journey from birth to enlightenment. This powerful sequence is based on the unique combination of Gene Keys that are most active in your Hologenetic Profile, which is determined by the specific time, date, and location of your birth. By understanding and working with your Activation Sequence, you can gain deep insight into the challenges, opportunities, and potential for transformation that lie ahead of you.

1. The Shadow (Birth to Age 35-40):

The first stage of the Activation Sequence, known as the Shadow, encompasses the first half of your life, typically from birth until around the age of 35 to 40. During this period, you are primarily engaged in a process of confronting and working through the limiting patterns, beliefs, and behaviors that hold you back from expressing your true potential. These shadows are the result of conditioned responses, traumas, and unresolved issues that have been passed down through your ancestral lineage and reinforced by your early life experiences.

Navigating the Shadow stage can be a challenging and often painful process, as you are forced to confront your deepest fears, wounds, and obstacles head-on. However, this process of facing and integrating your shadows is essential for personal growth and transformation. By shining the light of awareness on these dark places within yourself, you begin to loosen the grip of unconscious patterns and create space for new possibilities to emerge.

During the Shadow stage, you may find yourself repeatedly drawn into difficult situations or relationships that trigger your core wounds and insecurities. While these experiences can be incredibly challenging, they also offer profound opportunities for healing and growth. By learning to meet your shadows with curiosity, compassion, and courage, you lay the foundation for the next stage of your journey.

2. The Gift (Age 35-40 to Age 50-55):

As you begin to transform and integrate your shadows, you enter the second stage of the Activation Sequence, known as the Gift. This stage typically unfolds between the ages of 35 to 40 and 50 to 55, and is characterized by a gradual awakening to the unique talents, capacities, and contributions that are encoded in your Gene Keys.

During the Gift stage, you start to experience a greater sense of purpose, creativity, and fulfillment as you align your life with your true essence and potential. The gifts that emerge during this period are not random or accidental, but rather are the direct result of the deep inner work you have done in confronting and integrating your shadows.

As you step more fully into your gifts, you may find that doors begin to open in synchronistic ways, leading you towards new opportunities and experiences that are in alignment with your highest potential. You may also find that your relationships become more harmonious and fulfilling, as you learn to express your authentic self and communicate your needs and boundaries with greater clarity and compassion.

The Gift stage is a time of great growth and expansion, as you begin to tap into the vast reservoir of potential that lies within you. By nurturing and expressing your unique gifts, you not only experience greater joy and fulfillment in your own life, but also make a positive impact on the world around you.

3. The Siddhi (Age 50-55 and Beyond):

The final stage of the Activation Sequence, known as the Siddhi, represents the highest frequency expression of your Gene Keys. This stage typically begins around the age of 50 to 55 and continues for the rest of your life, as you fully embody and integrate the lessons and insights of the previous stages.

During the Siddhi stage, you may experience profound states of wisdom, compassion, and unity consciousness, as you awaken to the deeper truths and mysteries of existence. The siddhis are not supernatural powers or abilities, but rather are the natural expression of a fully realized and enlightened being.

As you anchor yourself in the siddhis of your Gene Keys, you become a living embodiment of love, wisdom, and service, radiating these qualities out into the world through your presence and actions. You may find that your life becomes a powerful catalyst for transformation and awakening, as you inspire and support others on their own journeys of growth and self-discovery.

The Siddhi stage is a time of great fulfillment and purpose, as you align your life with the highest expression of your being. While the journey to this stage is not always easy, it is a path of profound beauty, meaning, and significance, offering a glimpse of the limitless potential that lies within each of us.

The Activation Sequence provides a powerful and illuminating framework for understanding the unfolding of your life's journey, from the challenges and shadows of your early years to the gifts and siddhis of your later life. By working with this sequence and integrating its insights and practices into your daily life, you can accelerate your own process of growth and transformation, and step more fully into the magnificent being you truly are.

The Venus Sequence

The Venus Sequence is a profound and transformative aspect of the Gene Keys system, focusing on the realm of relationships and love. This sequence is based on the specific Gene Keys that are active in your Venus Profile, which is determined by the position of the planet Venus at the precise moment of your birth. By exploring and working with your Venus Sequence, you can gain deep insight into the patterns, challenges, and opportunities that arise in your connections with others, as well as your relationship with yourself.

1. The Shadow:

In the shadow stage of the Venus Sequence, you may find yourself confronting various challenges and obstacles in your relationships. These shadows can manifest as patterns of codependency, where you may struggle to maintain healthy boundaries and prioritize your own needs and desires. You may also experience a deep-seated fear of intimacy, which can prevent you from fully opening your heart and allowing yourself to be vulnerable with others. Additionally, you may grapple with issues of trust and vulnerability, finding it difficult to let your guard down and fully embrace the depth of connection that relationships offer.

2. The Gift:

As you begin to illuminate and transform your relationship shadows, you unlock access to the profound gifts of the Venus Sequence. One of the key gifts that emerges is the capacity for deep empathy and understanding. You may find yourself naturally attuned to the emotions and experiences of others, able to hold space for their struggles and triumphs with an open heart. Another gift of this stage is the ability to express and embody compassion, not only towards others but also towards yourself. You learn to extend kindness and understanding to all aspects of your being, embracing your own humanity with tenderness and grace. The ultimate gift of the Venus Sequence is the experience of unconditional love – a love that transcends the limitations of the ego and embraces the inherent divinity within all beings.

3. The Siddhi:

In the siddhi stage of the Venus Sequence, you may find yourself entering into profound states of unity, bliss, and spiritual partnership. As you fully embody the gifts of empathy, compassion, and unconditional love, you begin to experience a deep sense of oneness with all of creation. The boundaries between self and other dissolve, revealing the fundamental interconnectedness of all beings. You may also find yourself experiencing states of ecstatic bliss, as the energy of love flows freely through your being, unencumbered by the limitations of the ego. In this stage, your relationships take on a sacred and transformative quality, becoming vehicles for mutual growth, healing, and awakening. You may attract and cultivate spiritual partnerships that support you in your highest unfolding, and that contribute to the greater good of all beings.

By working with the Venus Sequence, you embark on a profound journey of self-discovery and transformation in the realm of relationships and love. As you navigate the shadows, cultivate the gifts, and embody the siddhis of this sequence, you deepen your capacity for authentic connection, intimacy, and unconditional love. You learn to create relationships that are rooted in truth, compassion, and mutual support, and that reflect the highest possibilities of human connection. Ultimately, the Venus Sequence invites you to experience the transformative power of love in all areas of your life, and to become a living embodiment of the divine essence that lies at the heart of all beings.

The Pearl Sequence

The Pearl Sequence is a transformative path within the Gene Keys system that focuses on the realm of prosperity and material abundance. This sequence is based on the specific Gene Keys that are active in your Pearl Profile, which is determined by the position of the Moon at the time of your birth. By exploring and working with your Pearl Sequence, you can gain valuable insights into your relationship with money, success, and the material world, and discover new ways to align your outer life with your inner spiritual journey.

1. The Shadow:

In the shadow stage of the Pearl Sequence, you may find yourself grappling with various challenges and limitations related to abundance and prosperity. One common shadow is the scarcity mentality, which is characterized by a deep-seated belief that there is not enough to go around. This mindset can lead to feelings of fear, lack, and competition, and can prevent you from fully embracing and enjoying the richness of life. Another shadow that may arise is the fear of failure, which can hold you back from taking risks and pursuing your dreams. You may also struggle with receiving abundance, feeling unworthy or undeserving of the good things that come your way.

2. The Gift:

As you begin to illuminate and transform your prosperity shadows, you unlock access to the remarkable gifts of the Pearl Sequence. One of the key gifts that emerges is a deep sense of creativity and innovation. You may find yourself naturally attuned to new ideas and possibilities, able to think outside the box and generate novel solutions to challenges. Another gift of this stage is the ability to manifest your desires and intentions with ease and grace. You learn to harness the power of your thoughts and emotions to create the life you truly want. The ultimate gift of the Pearl Sequence is the experience of true wealth – a wealth that goes beyond mere financial abundance and encompasses a deep sense of fulfillment, purpose, and meaning.

3. The Siddhi:

In the siddhi stage of the Pearl Sequence, you may find yourself entering into profound states of grace, ease, and flow in your material life. As you fully embody the gifts of creativity, manifestation, and true wealth, you begin to experience a deep sense of alignment and synchronicity with the natural rhythms of the universe. Opportunities and resources seem to flow to you effortlessly, as if guided by an unseen hand. You may also find yourself experiencing a profound sense of trust and surrender, knowing that all of your needs are always met in perfect timing. In this stage, your material life becomes a reflection of your spiritual path, a sacred dance of giving and receiving, manifestation and release.

By working with the Pearl Sequence, you embark on a profound journey of transformation and awakening in the realm of prosperity and abundance. As you navigate the shadows, cultivate the gifts, and embody the siddhis of this sequence, you learn to create a life of true wealth and fulfillment, one that is aligned with your deepest values and aspirations. You discover that true prosperity is not just about accumulating material resources, but about living in harmony with the natural flow of life, and expressing your unique gifts and talents in service to the world. Ultimately, the Pearl Sequence invites you to experience the profound joy and freedom that comes from living a life of purpose, passion, and abundance, and to become a shining example of the limitless potential that lies within each of us.

Summary

The three sequences of Gene Keys — the Activation Sequence, the Venus Sequence, and the Pearl Sequence — provide a comprehensive framework for personal growth and transformation. By exploring these sequences and working with your own Gene Keys, you can gain deep insight into your life's journey, your relationships, and your path of prosperity.

Remember that these sequences are not linear or fixed — they are fluid and interconnected, weaving together to create the tapestry of your unique experience. As you embark on your journey with Gene Keys, trust in the wisdom and timing of your own unfolding, and allow these powerful teachings to guide and support you along the way.

In the next chapter, we'll explore the many benefits of Gene Keys readings, and how they can support you in cultivating greater self-awareness, authenticity, and fulfillment in all areas of your life.

Jenna Parker

Chapter 3: The Benefits of Gene Keys Readings

As you embark on your journey with Gene Keys, you may be wondering what benefits you can expect to receive from this transformative system.

In this chapter, we'll explore the many ways that Gene Keys readings can support you in cultivating greater self-awareness, personal growth, and fulfillment in all areas of your life.

Insight into Your Strengths and Challenges
One of the primary benefits of Gene Keys readings is the insight they provide into your unique strengths, gifts, and challenges. By exploring your Hologenetic Profile, you can gain a deep understanding of the specific Gene Keys that are most active in your life, and how they influence your personality, behavior, and life experiences.

This insight can be incredibly empowering, as it allows you to identify and cultivate your natural talents and abilities, while also illuminating the areas where you may face challenges or obstacles. By working with your Gene Keys, you can develop greater self-awareness and self-acceptance, and learn to harness your strengths in service of your highest potential.

Personal Growth and Transformation

One of the most significant and transformative benefits of exploring your Gene Keys is the incredible opportunity for personal growth and positive change. The Gene Keys system is thoughtfully designed to guide you on a profound journey of self-discovery, helping you navigate the path from shadow to gift to siddhi. By embarking on this journey, you unlock the door to your full potential, allowing you to live a life filled with greater purpose, passion, and deep fulfillment.

At the heart of the Gene Keys teachings is the concept of the shadow – the limiting patterns, beliefs, and behaviors that hold you back from expressing your true, authentic self. These shadows often manifest as fears, doubts, or feelings of unworthiness that can prevent you from reaching for your dreams and living the life you truly desire. However, the Gene Keys system views these shadows not as obstacles to be overcome, but as powerful opportunities for growth and transformation.

By courageously confronting and working with your shadows, you begin to alchemize them into gifts – the unique talents, qualities, and strengths that lie hidden within you. This process of transformation is not always easy, as it requires you to face your deepest fears and insecurities head-on. However, with the guidance and support of the Gene Keys, you can navigate this challenging terrain with greater ease, grace, and clarity.

As you continue on your journey of transformation, you may begin to experience the emergence of siddhis – the highest expression of your gifts and the ultimate realization of your true potential. Siddhis represent a state of being characterized by profound wisdom, unconditional love, and a deep sense of unity with all of life. When you embody your siddhis, you become a beacon of light and inspiration for others, effortlessly sharing your unique gifts with the world.

An Introduction to The Gene Keys

The Gene Keys provide a powerful framework for personal growth and transformation, offering a step-by-step guide to help you unlock your full potential. Through the insights gained from your Gene Keys readings, you'll discover practical tools, techniques, and practices that support you in navigating the ups and downs of your transformative journey. Whether you're seeking to overcome personal challenges, develop new skills and talents, or simply live a more authentic and fulfilling life, the Gene Keys system meets you where you are and helps you take the next steps forward.

As you delve deeper into your Gene Keys, you may find that the journey of transformation extends far beyond your own personal growth. The changes you experience within yourself have a ripple effect, positively impacting your relationships, your work, and the world around you. By doing the inner work to transform your shadows and embody your gifts, you contribute to the collective awakening of humanity, helping to create a world that is more compassionate, loving, and alive.

The path of personal growth and transformation through the Gene Keys is a lifelong journey, one that requires courage, commitment, and a willingness to embrace change. However, the rewards of this journey are immeasurable – a life filled with purpose, joy, and the deep satisfaction of knowing that you are living in alignment with your highest truth. With the Gene Keys as your guide, you can step boldly onto the path of transformation, trust in the wisdom of your own unfolding, and discover the extraordinary beauty and potential that lies within you.

Deepening Self-Awareness and Self-Compassion

One of the most profound benefits of Gene Keys readings is the way they can deepen your sense of self-awareness and self-compassion. By exploring your own unique patterns and tendencies, you can develop a greater understanding of your own psyche and emotional landscape, and learn to relate to yourself with greater kindness, patience, and understanding.

The Gene Keys teachings emphasize the importance of self-love and self-acceptance, recognizing that our shadows and challenges are not obstacles to be overcome, but rather, opportunities for growth and transformation. By learning to embrace and work with all aspects of yourself — including your fears, doubts, and limitations — you can cultivate a greater sense of wholeness and integration.

Through this process of self-discovery and self-compassion, you may find that you develop a greater capacity for empathy, both for yourself and for others. As you learn to accept and love yourself more fully, you may naturally extend that same compassion and understanding to those around you, leading to more harmonious and fulfilling relationships.

Enhancing Relationships and Communication

Speaking of relationships, another key benefit of Gene Keys readings is the way they can enhance your interpersonal connections and communication skills. The Venus Sequence, in particular, is focused on the path of love and relationships, and can provide valuable insights into your unique relationship patterns and challenges.

By exploring your Venus Profile, you can gain a deeper understanding of your own needs, desires, and tendencies in relationships, as well as the ways in which you may be unconsciously sabotaging or limiting your connections with others. With this awareness, you can begin to cultivate more authentic, compassionate, and fulfilling relationships, both with romantic partners and with friends, family members, and colleagues.

Additionally, the Gene Keys teachings can support you in developing greater empathy, emotional intelligence, and communication skills. By learning to listen deeply to yourself and others, to express your needs and boundaries with clarity and compassion, and to navigate conflict with greater skill and understanding, you can create more harmonious and supportive relationships in all areas of your life.

Spiritual Growth and Enlightenment

At the heart of the Gene Keys system lies a profound invitation to embark on a transformative journey of spiritual growth and enlightenment. While the Gene Keys offer invaluable insights and tools for personal development and self-discovery, their true power lies in their ability to guide you toward the ultimate realization of your highest potential – the discovery of your true nature and the awakening of your divine essence.

The path of spiritual growth and enlightenment through the Gene Keys is one of deep inner exploration, requiring a willingness to engage in the practices of contemplation, meditation, and self-inquiry. These practices serve as the foundation for the journey of transformation, allowing you to gradually peel back the layers of conditioning and illusion that obscure your true self.

As you work with your Gene Keys and navigate the journey from shadow to gift to siddhi, you begin to access the deeper dimensions of your being. You may find yourself experiencing profound states of wisdom, compassion, and unity consciousness – states that reveal the interconnectedness of all life and the inherent divinity within all things.

This process of spiritual awakening is not always easy, as it requires you to confront and release the limiting beliefs, patterns, and identities that have defined your sense of self for so long. However, with the guidance and support of the Gene Keys, you can navigate this transformative terrain with greater courage, resilience, and grace.

As you continue on your path of spiritual growth, you may begin to notice subtle shifts in your perception and experience of reality. The veil of separation between yourself and others begins to thin, revealing the underlying unity and oneness that pervades all of existence. You may find yourself naturally gravitating towards a greater sense of purpose, meaning, and connection, as you align your life with the greater web of life.

The ultimate goal of the Gene Keys journey is the realization of enlightenment – the direct experience of your true nature as pure, boundless awareness. This is a state of being that transcends the limitations of the ego and the mind, revealing the infinite potential and creativity that lies within you.

While the path to enlightenment is unique for each individual, the Gene Keys provide a powerful framework and set of tools to support you on your journey. Through the practice of contemplation, you can deepen your understanding of the Gene Keys and their corresponding shadow, gift, and siddhi frequencies. By meditating on these frequencies and allowing them to resonate within your being, you gradually attune yourself to higher states of consciousness and awareness.

Self-inquiry is another essential practice on the path of spiritual growth and enlightenment. By turning your attention inward and questioning the nature of your thoughts, beliefs, and identities, you begin to unravel the knots of conditioning that keep you bound to a limited sense of self. As you inquire deeper into the nature of your being, you may experience profound insights and revelations that transform your understanding of yourself and the world around you.

It's important to approach the journey of spiritual growth and enlightenment with patience, compassion, and a sense of surrender. The path is not always linear, and there may be times when you feel like you are taking steps backward or getting lost along the way. However, by trusting in the wisdom of your own unfolding and the guidance of your Gene Keys, you can navigate the ups and downs of the journey with greater ease and grace.

Ultimately, the path of spiritual growth and enlightenment is a journey of coming home to yourself – of discovering the innate beauty, wisdom, and love that lies at the core of your being. Through the Gene Keys, you are invited to embark on this transformative journey, to shed the layers of illusion that separate you from your true nature, and to awaken to the extraordinary potential that lies within you. By dedicating yourself to this path, you open yourself up to the possibility of profound spiritual growth, enlightenment, and a new way of being in the world – one characterized by greater purpose, meaning, and connection to all of life.

Summary

In this chapter, we've explored the many benefits of Gene Keys readings, from gaining insight into your strengths and challenges, to cultivating personal growth and transformation, to deepening your self-awareness and self-compassion, to enhancing your relationships and communication skills, to supporting your spiritual growth and enlightenment.

As you continue on your journey with Gene Keys, remember that the path of transformation is not always easy, but it is always worth it. Trust in the wisdom and guidance of your own unique Gene Keys, and allow them to support you in unlocking your full potential and living a life of greater purpose, passion, and fulfillment.

In the next chapter, we'll dive deeper into the process of interpreting your own Hologenetic Profile, and explore some practical tools and techniques for working with your Gene Keys on a daily basis.

Chapter 4: Interpreting Your Hologenetic Profile

Now that you have a deeper understanding of the benefits and potential of Gene Keys, you may be eager to dive into your own Hologenetic Profile and start exploring your unique path of transformation.

In this chapter, we'll guide you through the process of obtaining and interpreting your Hologenetic Profile, and provide some practical examples and techniques for working with your Gene Keys on a daily basis.

Obtaining Your Hologenetic Profile

The journey of self-discovery and transformation through the Gene Keys begins with obtaining your personalized Hologenetic Profile. This unique profile is a comprehensive map of your individual genetic blueprint, revealing the specific Gene Keys that are most active and influential in your life. By understanding and working with these Gene Keys, you can unlock a wealth of insights and guidance that can support you in navigating your path of growth and evolution.

Your Hologenetic Profile is based on the precise details of your birth – your date, time, and place of entry into this world. These details are not seen as mere coincidences within the Gene Keys system, but rather as a reflection of the greater cosmic intelligence that underlies all of life. Just as a seed contains within it the blueprint for the fully grown tree, your birth details contain within them the blueprint for your unique journey of unfolding.

To obtain your Hologenetic Profile, the first step is to visit the official Gene Keys website. Here, you'll find a variety of profile options and readings available for purchase. The most comprehensive option is the full Hologenetic Profile, which includes an in-depth analysis of your Activation Sequence, Venus Sequence, and Pearl Sequence.

Your Activation Sequence is the foundation of your Hologenetic Profile, representing the unique path of transformation that you'll navigate throughout your life. This sequence reveals the specific Gene Keys that will be most active and influential in your journey, and provides a roadmap for your growth and evolution from shadow to gift to siddhi.

The Venus Sequence is an additional layer of your profile that focuses specifically on your relationships and the way you relate to others and the world around you. This sequence reveals the Gene Keys that are most active in your heart center, and offers guidance on how to cultivate more harmonious, loving, and authentic connections in your life.

The Pearl Sequence is the final layer of your Hologenetic Profile, representing your unique path of prosperity and material manifestation. This sequence reveals the Gene Keys that are most active in your throat center, and provides insights on how to align your creative expression and material life with your highest purpose and potential.

When you purchase your Hologenetic Profile reading, you'll receive a detailed report that includes a wealth of information about each of these sequences and the specific Gene Keys that are most active in your life. This report is not just a static document, but a dynamic tool that you can work with over time to deepen your understanding of yourself and your path.

An Introduction to The Gene Keys

The report begins with an overview of your Hologenetic Profile, including a summary of your primary Gene Keys and their corresponding shadow, gift, and siddhi frequencies. From there, the report delves into each of your sequences in detail, offering in-depth descriptions of the Gene Keys that are most active in each sequence and how they relate to your unique path of transformation.

In addition to the written descriptions, your Hologenetic Profile report also includes a variety of visual aids and diagrams that can help you to better understand and integrate the information. These may include color-coded maps of your Gene Keys, as well as images and symbols that correspond to the different frequencies and themes of your profile.

One of the most valuable aspects of your Hologenetic Profile report is the practical guidance and suggestions it offers for working with your Gene Keys on a daily basis. This may include specific contemplations, meditations, and exercises that can help you to activate and integrate the wisdom of your Gene Keys into your life.

It's important to approach your Hologenetic Profile with a sense of openness and curiosity, rather than as a fixed blueprint or prediction of your life path. Your profile is a tool for self-discovery and transformation, not a prescription for how your life should unfold. By engaging with your profile in a spirit of exploration and experimentation, you can unlock its true power and potential.

Obtaining your Hologenetic Profile is an essential first step on the journey of self-discovery and transformation through the Gene Keys. By investing in this powerful tool, you are making a commitment to your own growth and evolution, and opening yourself up to a wealth of insights, guidance, and support that can help you to navigate your unique path with greater ease, grace, and clarity. With your Hologenetic Profile as your guide, you can begin to unlock the full potential of your being, and create a life that is truly aligned with your highest purpose and potential.

Interpreting Your Profile

Once you have your Hologenetic Profile in hand, the next step is to begin interpreting and working with your Gene Keys. This can feel like a daunting task at first, but with a little guidance and practice, you'll soon be able to navigate your profile with ease and confidence.

The first thing to understand about your Hologenetic Profile is that it is divided into three main sections: the Activation Sequence, the Venus Sequence, and the Pearl Sequence. Each of these sequences represents a different aspect of your life and consciousness, and provides insight into your unique path of transformation.

Let's take a closer look at each of these sequences:

The Activation Sequence

Your Activation Sequence is based on the Gene Keys that were active at the moment of your birth, and represents your life's journey from shadow to gift to siddhi. This sequence is divided into three main sections:

1. The Sphere of Consciousness: This section represents your overall life purpose and the unique gifts and challenges that you are here to work with in this lifetime.

2. The Line: This section represents your life's journey from birth to death, and is divided into six stages, each corresponding to a different Gene Key.

3. The Shadow, Gift, and Siddhi: For each Gene Key in your Activation Sequence, you will see a description of the shadow, gift, and siddhi frequencies. These frequencies represent the spectrum of potential within each Gene Key, from the lowest to the highest expression.

To interpret your Activation Sequence, start by exploring your Sphere of Consciousness and the overall themes and patterns that emerge. Then, look at each of the six stages of your Line, and consider how the shadow, gift, and siddhi frequencies of each Gene Key may be manifesting in your life at different times and in different areas.

The Venus Sequence

Your Venus Sequence is based on the Gene Keys that were active at the moment of your birth in relation to the position of Venus, and represents your unique path of love and relationships. Like the Activation Sequence, the Venus Sequence is divided into three main sections:

1. The Sphere of Relationships: This section represents your overall relationship style and the unique gifts and challenges that you bring to your connections with others.

2. The Line: This section represents your journey through different stages and types of relationships, from early childhood bonds to romantic partnerships to spiritual connections.

3. The Shadow, Gift, and Siddhi: For each Gene Key in your Venus Sequence, you will see a description of the shadow, gift, and siddhi frequencies, representing the spectrum of potential within each Gene Key as it relates to love and relationships.

To interpret your Venus Sequence, start by exploring your Sphere of Relationships and the overall themes and patterns that emerge. Then, look at each of the stages of your Line, and consider how the shadow, gift, and siddhi frequencies of each Gene Key may be manifesting in your relationships at different times and in different ways.

The Pearl Sequence

Your Pearl Sequence is based on the Gene Keys that were active at the moment of your birth in relation to the position of the Moon, and represents your unique path of prosperity and material abundance. Like the other sequences, the Pearl Sequence is divided into three main sections:

1. The Sphere of Prosperity: This section represents your overall relationship with money, success, and material reality, and the unique gifts and challenges that you bring to this area of your life.

2. The Line: This section represents your journey through different stages and aspects of prosperity, from your early experiences with money and resources to your ultimate potential for true wealth and abundance.

3. The Shadow, Gift, and Siddhi: For each Gene Key in your Pearl Sequence, you will see a description of the shadow, gift, and siddhi frequencies, representing the spectrum of potential within each Gene Key as it relates to prosperity and material success.

To interpret your Pearl Sequence, start by exploring your Sphere of Prosperity and the overall themes and patterns that emerge. Then, look at each of the stages of your Line, and consider how the shadow, gift, and siddhi frequencies of each Gene Key may be manifesting in your relationship with money and success at different times and in different ways.

Putting It All Together

As you work with your Hologenetic Profile, it's important to remember that these sequences are not separate or isolated from one another, but rather, are interconnected and mutually informing. Your Activation Sequence provides the overall context and foundation for your life's journey, while your Venus and Pearl Sequences offer specific insight into the areas of relationships and prosperity.

To get the most out of your Hologenetic Profile, try to approach it with a spirit of curiosity, openness, and self-compassion. Remember that your Gene Keys are not fixed or deterministic, but rather, are invitations to explore and embrace the full spectrum of your potential. By working with your shadows, cultivating your gifts, and embodying your siddhis, you can transform your life and create a deeper sense of purpose, fulfillment, and joy.

Practical Examples and Techniques

To help you get started with interpreting and working with your Hologenetic Profile, here are a few practical examples and techniques:

1. Contemplation:

One of the most powerful ways to work with your Gene Keys is through the practice of contemplation. Choose a specific Gene Key from your profile, and spend some time each day sitting with the shadow, gift, and siddhi frequencies. Allow yourself to explore the full spectrum of potential within this Gene Key, and notice any insights, emotions, or sensations that arise.

2. Journaling:

Another helpful technique is to keep a Gene Keys journal, where you can record your experiences, insights, and reflections as you work with your profile. You might choose to focus on a specific sequence or Gene Key each week or month, and use your journal to track your progress and growth over time.

3. Affirmations:

You can also use affirmations to help you embody the higher frequencies of your Gene Keys. For example, if you are working with the gift frequency of a particular Gene Key, you might create an affirmation that reflects this quality, such as "I am compassionate and understanding in my relationships" or "I trust in the abundance and generosity of the universe."

4. Visualization:

Finally, visualization can be a powerful tool for working with your Gene Keys. You might choose to visualize yourself embodying the siddhi frequency of a particular Gene Key, or creating a life that reflects the highest potential of your Hologenetic Profile. Allow yourself to fully immerse in the experience, and trust in the transformative power of your imagination.

Summary

In this chapter, we've explored the process of interpreting your Hologenetic Profile, and provided some practical examples and techniques for working with your Gene Keys on a daily basis. Remember that this is a lifelong journey of growth and transformation, and that your Hologenetic Profile is a powerful tool to support you along the way.

As you continue to work with your Gene Keys, trust in the wisdom and guidance of your own inner knowing, and allow yourself to be open to the full spectrum of your potential. Whether you are just beginning your journey or are a seasoned practitioner, the Gene Keys offer a rich and rewarding path of self-discovery and transformation.

In the next chapter, we'll explore some of the common challenges and obstacles that can arise as you work with your Gene Keys, and offer some guidance and support for navigating these challenges with grace and resilience.

Jenna Parker

Chapter 5: Practical Applications of Gene Keys

Now that you have a solid understanding of your Hologenetic Profile and how to interpret it, you may be wondering how to apply this knowledge in your daily life.

In this chapter, we'll explore some practical ways to integrate Gene Keys into your personal growth and spiritual evolution, and provide exercises and techniques to support you on your journey.

Self-Discovery and Personal Development

One of the primary applications of Gene Keys is as a tool for self-discovery and personal development. By working with your Hologenetic Profile, you can gain deeper insight into your unique strengths, challenges, and opportunities for growth, and use this knowledge to create a more authentic and fulfilling life.

Here are a few specific ways you can use Gene Keys for self-discovery and personal development:

1. Identifying your purpose:

Your Activation Sequence can provide valuable insight into your overall life purpose and the unique gifts and talents you are here to share with the world. By exploring your Sphere of Consciousness and the Gene Keys in your Line, you can gain clarity on your true calling and begin to align your life with your deepest values and aspirations.

2. Overcoming limiting patterns:

Your shadows represent the limiting patterns, beliefs, and behaviors that can hold you back from expressing your full potential. By bringing awareness to these shadows and working to transform them, you can break free from old habits and create new possibilities for growth and change.

3. Cultivating your gifts:

Your gifts represent your unique strengths and talents, and the qualities that come most naturally to you. By identifying and nurturing these gifts, you can build greater confidence, creativity, and resilience, and share your unique contributions with the world.

4. Embodying your siddhis:

Your siddhis represent the highest potential of your Gene Keys, and the states of consciousness that are available to you as you evolve and grow. By contemplating and embodying these siddhis, you can experience greater wisdom, compassion, and unity, and live a life of profound purpose and meaning.

Spiritual Evolution and Enlightenment

In addition to supporting personal development, Gene Keys can also be a powerful tool for spiritual evolution and enlightenment.

An Introduction to The Gene Keys

The Gene Keys teachings are rooted in a deep understanding of the nature of consciousness and the journey of awakening, and offer a framework for navigating this journey with grace and wisdom.

Here are a few specific ways you can use Gene Keys for spiritual evolution and enlightenment:

1. Contemplation and meditation:

Contemplation and meditation are foundational practices within the Gene Keys system, offering a powerful means to cultivate greater awareness, insight, and inner peace. By dedicating time each day to deep reflection and meditation on the shadow, gift, and siddhi frequencies of your Gene Keys, you can begin to access the wisdom and guidance of your own inner knowing.

The practice of contemplation involves holding a specific Gene Key or frequency in your awareness, and allowing yourself to be present with whatever arises in response. This may include thoughts, emotions, sensations, or insights that emerge from the depths of your being. By approaching contemplation with a sense of open curiosity and non-judgment, you can begin to unravel the layers of conditioning and belief that obscure your true nature.

Meditation, on the other hand, involves cultivating a state of deep inner stillness and presence. By focusing your attention on the breath, a mantra, or the sensations in your body, you can begin to quiet the mind and access a space of pure awareness. From this space, you can observe the play of your thoughts and emotions with greater clarity and detachment, and begin to experience the underlying unity and interconnectedness of all things.

Through regular practice of contemplation and meditation, you can deepen your understanding of your Gene Keys and their corresponding frequencies, and open yourself to the wisdom and guidance of your own inner teacher. As you become more attuned to the subtle energies and insights that arise in these practices, you may find that you naturally begin to embody the qualities of your Gene Keys in your daily life, and experience a greater sense of alignment and flow.

2. Integrating shadow work:

Shadow work is a crucial aspect of the Gene Keys journey, and involves bringing conscious awareness to the limiting patterns, beliefs, and behaviors that can hold you back from expressing your full potential. These shadows often manifest as fears, doubts, or feelings of unworthiness that can prevent you from fully embracing your gifts and embodying your highest truth.

Integrating shadow work requires a willingness to face these challenging aspects of yourself with honesty, compassion, and courage. Rather than trying to suppress or ignore your shadows, the Gene Keys teachings invite you to approach them with a sense of curiosity and openness, acknowledging them as an integral part of your being.

By shining the light of awareness on your shadows, you begin to loosen their grip on your psyche and create space for new possibilities to emerge. This process can be uncomfortable or even painful at times, as it requires you to confront the parts of yourself that you may have long denied or rejected. However, by embracing your shadows and allowing them to be seen and felt fully, you can begin to alchemize them into gifts and siddhis.

The integration of shadow work is a lifelong journey, and one that requires ongoing commitment and practice. As you work with your Gene Keys and navigate the path from shadow to gift to siddhi, you may find that new layers of shadow emerge, inviting you to go deeper into the process of self-discovery and transformation. By approaching this work with patience, self-compassion, and a willingness to surrender to the unfolding of your own unique journey, you can experience greater wholeness, integration, and freedom on your spiritual path.

3. Cultivating higher states of consciousness:

The siddhis of Gene Keys represent the highest states of consciousness available to us as human beings, and include qualities such as unity, enlightenment, and unconditional love. These states are not seen as distant or unattainable within the Gene Keys system, but rather as the natural expression of our true nature, waiting to be realized and embodied.

Cultivating higher states of consciousness through the Gene Keys involves a commitment to ongoing contemplation, meditation, and embodiment of the siddhi frequencies. By regularly attuning yourself to these frequencies and allowing them to resonate within your being, you begin to anchor them in your consciousness and experience.

This process of cultivation is not always easy, as it requires a willingness to let go of the limiting beliefs, identities, and patterns that keep you bound to a sense of separation and lack. However, as you deepen your practice and allow the siddhis to permeate your being, you may begin to experience profound shifts in your perception and understanding of reality.

These shifts may manifest as a growing sense of unity and interconnectedness with all of life, a deep appreciation for the beauty and perfection of existence, and a natural expression of unconditional love and compassion for all beings. As you embody the siddhis more fully, you may find that your actions and relationships naturally align with these higher qualities, and that you become a powerful catalyst for transformation in the world around you.

Ultimately, the cultivation of higher states of consciousness through the Gene Keys is a journey of remembrance – of awakening to the truth of who you are beyond the limitations of the mind and ego. By dedicating yourself to this path and surrendering to the wisdom of your own inner guidance, you can experience a profound sense of liberation, fulfillment, and alignment with the greater unfolding of life.

4. Connecting with community:

One of the great gifts of the Gene Keys system is the global community of individuals who are committed to personal and collective transformation. This community spans a wide range of ages, backgrounds, and cultures, united by a shared intention to awaken to their highest potential and contribute to the evolution of consciousness on the planet.

Connecting with the Gene Keys community can be a powerful support and catalyst for your own journey of spiritual evolution and enlightenment. By joining online forums, attending local meetups or events, or participating in group courses or retreats, you can find inspiration, guidance, and reflection from others who are walking a similar path.

Within the Gene Keys community, you may find opportunities to share your own insights and experiences, and to learn from the wisdom and perspectives of others. You may also find resonance with specific individuals or groups who share your particular interests or challenges, and who can offer targeted support and guidance for your journey.

In addition to the practical benefits of community connection, engaging with the Gene Keys community can also be a profound spiritual practice in itself. By opening yourself to the reflections and mirrors that others provide, you can gain deeper insight into your own patterns and blind spots, and accelerate your process of growth and transformation.

At a deeper level, connecting with the Gene Keys community can also be a powerful reminder of the inherent unity and interconnectedness of all beings. By recognizing the shared humanity and divinity in others, you begin to dissolve the illusion of separation and isolation, and experience a greater sense of belonging and purpose in the world.

As you deepen your engagement with the Gene Keys community and allow yourself to be both a giver and receiver of support and wisdom, you may find that your own journey of spiritual evolution and enlightenment takes on a new depth and dimension. By walking the path in the company of others, you can experience the joy and fulfillment of co-creating a world that reflects the highest potential of the human spirit.

Exercises and Techniques

To help you integrate Gene Keys into your daily life and spiritual practice, here are a few exercises and techniques to try:

1. Daily contemplation:

One of the most powerful ways to work with your Gene Keys is through the practice of daily contemplation. This involves choosing a specific Gene Key from your Hologenetic Profile and dedicating a set amount of time each day to deep reflection and meditation on its shadow, gift, and siddhi frequencies.

To begin, find a quiet space where you can sit comfortably and undisturbed for 5-10 minutes. Take a few deep breaths to center yourself and let go of any distractions or preoccupations. Then, bring your chosen Gene Key to mind, either by visualizing its corresponding symbol or simply holding its essence in your awareness.

As you sit with the Gene Key, allow yourself to be present with whatever arises in response. This may include thoughts, emotions, sensations, or insights that emerge from the depths of your being. Rather than trying to analyze or interpret these experiences, simply allow them to be, and notice any patterns or themes that emerge.

You may find it helpful to focus on a particular aspect of the Gene Key that resonates with you, such as its shadow, gift, or siddhi frequency. Alternatively, you may simply allow your mind to rest in the essence of the Gene Key itself, without any specific focus or intention.

As you continue your practice of daily contemplation, you may find that your relationship with your Gene Keys deepens and evolves over time. By consistently showing up and allowing yourself to be present with these archetypal energies, you can begin to integrate their wisdom and guidance into your daily life, and experience a greater sense of alignment and purpose.

2. Journaling prompts:

In addition to contemplation, journaling can be a powerful tool for working with your Gene Keys and exploring the themes and patterns that emerge in your life. By using your Hologenetic Profile as a source of journaling prompts, you can gain deeper insight into your own experiences and challenges, and discover new ways of navigating them with grace and wisdom.

To begin, choose a specific sequence or Gene Key from your profile that feels particularly relevant or resonant for you at this time. You may want to focus on a Gene Key that corresponds to a current challenge or opportunity in your life, or one that simply sparks your curiosity and interest.

Once you have chosen your focus, take some time to reflect on the shadow, gift, and siddhi frequencies of that Gene Key, and how they may be manifesting in your current experiences. You may want to ask yourself questions such as:

- What limiting patterns or beliefs do I notice arising in relation to this Gene Key?
- How can I embrace and integrate the gifts and strengths of this Gene Key more fully?
- What would it look like to embody the siddhi frequency of this Gene Key in my daily life?

As you journal, allow yourself to write freely and without judgment, letting your thoughts and feelings flow onto the page. You may find that new insights and understandings emerge as you write, or that patterns and connections become clearer over time.

You may also want to experiment with different journaling formats and techniques, such as stream-of-consciousness writing, dialoguing with different aspects of yourself, or using visual aids like drawings or collages to explore your experiences more deeply.

By consistently engaging in this practice of reflective journaling, you can cultivate a deeper sense of self-awareness and self-compassion, and gain valuable insights and tools for navigating your unique path of growth and transformation.

3. Embodiment practices:

While much of the work with Gene Keys involves introspection and reflection, it is equally important to bring the teachings into your physical body and daily life. One powerful way to do this is through the practice of embodiment, which involves consciously engaging in activities and experiences that allow you to integrate and express the qualities and frequencies of your Gene Keys.

There are many different embodiment practices that you can explore, depending on your personal preferences and interests. Some examples include:

- Yoga: By engaging in specific yoga postures and sequences, you can cultivate the physical, emotional, and energetic qualities of your Gene Keys, such as strength, flexibility, balance, and flow.

- Dance: Free-form dance and movement can be a powerful way to express and release the energies and emotions associated with your Gene Keys, and to cultivate a sense of joy, creativity, and spontaneity.

- Martial arts: Practices like tai chi, qigong, and aikido can help you develop the qualities of groundedness, centeredness, and presence that are essential for embodying the higher frequencies of your Gene Keys.

- Breathwork: Conscious breathing practices can help you regulate your nervous system, release tension and stress, and cultivate a sense of inner peace and clarity that supports your work with the Gene Keys.

To begin an embodiment practice, you may want to choose a specific Gene Key that relates to a quality or theme you wish to cultivate, such as vitality, creativity, or compassion. Take some time to contemplate the shadow, gift, and siddhi frequencies of that Gene Key, and notice any physical sensations or impulses that arise in response.

Then, engage in your chosen embodiment practice with the intention of bringing those qualities and frequencies into your physical body and experience. You may want to focus on specific areas of your body that correspond to the Gene Key, or simply allow your body to move and express itself in whatever way feels natural and authentic.

As you continue to practice embodiment, you may find that the qualities and frequencies of your Gene Keys become more deeply integrated into your being, and that you are able to express them more fully and naturally in your daily life. Over time, this can lead to a greater sense of wholeness, vitality, and alignment with your true nature.

4. Dialogue and sharing:

One of the most valuable aspects of working with Gene Keys is the opportunity to connect with others who are on a similar path of growth and discovery. By engaging in regular dialogue and sharing with a friend, partner, or community member who is also interested in Gene Keys, you can deepen your understanding and integration of the teachings, and find support and inspiration for your journey.

To begin a Gene Keys dialogue, you may want to choose a specific theme or challenge that you are currently working with, and invite your partner to share their own experiences and insights related to that topic. You can use your Hologenetic Profiles as a starting point for exploration, comparing and contrasting your individual Gene Keys and how they may be influencing your experiences.

As you engage in dialogue, it is important to create a safe and supportive space for sharing, where both partners feel heard, respected, and understood. You may want to establish some basic guidelines or agreements, such as maintaining confidentiality, practicing active listening, and avoiding judgment or advice-giving.

Some questions or prompts that you may want to explore in your Gene Keys dialogues include:

- What shadow patterns or challenges are you currently working with, and how do they relate to your Gene Keys?
- What gifts or strengths are you discovering or cultivating, and how can you express them more fully in your life?
- What insights or revelations have you had about your life purpose or path, and how do they align with your Gene Keys?
- What practices or techniques have you found helpful for integrating and embodying the teachings of Gene Keys?

In addition to one-on-one dialogues, you may also want to explore group sharing or community discussions related to Gene Keys. Many online and in-person communities exist where individuals can come together to share their experiences, ask questions, and offer support and guidance to one another.

By engaging in regular dialogue and sharing with others who are working with Gene Keys, you can accelerate your own learning and growth, and contribute to the collective wisdom and evolution of the community as a whole. Over time, these connections can become a powerful source of inspiration, encouragement, and accountability on your journey of self-discovery and transformation.

Summary

In this chapter, we've explored some of the practical applications of Gene Keys, and provided exercises and techniques for integrating this powerful tool into your daily life and spiritual practice. Whether you are using Gene Keys for personal development, spiritual evolution, or both, the key is to approach the journey with an open heart and a willingness to learn and grow.

As you continue on your path with Gene Keys, remember that the journey is not always easy, but it is always worth it. Trust in the wisdom and guidance of your own inner knowing, and allow yourself to be open to the full spectrum of your potential. With patience, persistence, and a deep commitment to your own growth and evolution, you can transform your life and create a world of greater beauty, harmony, and love.

In the next chapter, we'll explore some of the common misunderstandings and misconceptions that can arise when working with Gene Keys, and provide clarity and guidance for navigating these challenges with grace and understanding.

Chapter 6: Common Misunderstandings of Gene Keys

As you delve deeper into the world of Gene Keys, you may encounter some common misunderstandings and misconceptions about this powerful system. These misunderstandings can create confusion, doubt, or even resistance on your path of growth and transformation. In this chapter, we'll identify and clarify some of the most common misunderstandings of Gene Keys, and provide guidance for navigating these challenges with clarity and understanding.

Misunderstanding 1: Gene Keys are deterministic or fatalistic

One of the most common misunderstandings of Gene Keys is the idea that they are deterministic or fatalistic – that is, that they predict or determine our fate or destiny in some fixed or unchangeable way. This misunderstanding can arise from the language of Gene Keys, which speaks of our "genetic heritage" and the "codes" that are embedded within us.

However, it's important to understand that Gene Keys are not about prediction or determination, but rather about potential and possibility. Your Hologenetic Profile is not a fixed blueprint for your life, but rather a map of the unique terrain of your inner landscape, with all its challenges, opportunities, and potentials.

The Gene Keys teachings emphasize that we always have the power to choose how we respond to the circumstances and conditions of our lives, and that our choices and actions can shape and transform our reality in profound ways. By working with your shadows and cultivating your gifts and siddhis, you can actively participate in your own growth and evolution, and create a life that reflects your deepest values and aspirations.

Misunderstanding 2: Shadows are negative traits to be eliminated

Another common misunderstanding of Gene Keys is the idea that our shadows are negative traits or flaws that need to be eliminated or overcome. This misunderstanding can create a sense of shame, judgment, or resistance around our shadows, and can prevent us from fully embracing and integrating these aspects of ourselves.

In reality, our shadows are not inherently negative or problematic, but rather are simply the undeveloped or unconscious aspects of our being that are calling for our attention and integration. Our shadows are the raw materials of our transformation, and by bringing awareness and compassion to these aspects of ourselves, we can alchemize them into gifts and siddhis.

The Gene Keys teachings emphasize that our shadows are not obstacles to be overcome, but rather are opportunities for growth and evolution. By embracing our shadows with curiosity and kindness, we can deepen our self-understanding and self-acceptance, and unlock the full potential of our being.

Misunderstanding 3: Gene Keys are only about individual growth

A third common misunderstanding of Gene Keys is the idea that they are solely focused on individual growth and transformation, and have little relevance or impact on the larger world or collective. This misunderstanding can create a sense of isolation or disconnection from the wider web of life, and can prevent us from fully appreciating the transformative power of Gene Keys.

In truth, the Gene Keys teachings are deeply rooted in a vision of collective healing and evolution, and recognize that our individual growth and transformation are intimately connected to the larger patterns and processes of life itself. As we work with our own shadows, gifts, and siddhis, we are not only transforming ourselves, but also contributing to the healing and evolution of the whole.

The Gene Keys community is a global network of individuals who are committed to personal and collective transformation, and who recognize that our individual journeys are part of a larger story of awakening and regeneration. By connecting with this community and engaging in collective practices and dialogues, we can deepen our understanding of the interdependence and interconnectedness of all life, and participate in the co-creation of a more just, sustainable, and compassionate world.

Guidance for navigating misunderstandings

If you find yourself encountering these or other misunderstandings of Gene Keys, here are a few pieces of guidance to keep in mind:

1. Embrace curiosity and openness:

Rather than getting caught in fixed ideas or assumptions about Gene Keys, approach the teachings with a spirit of curiosity and openness. Allow yourself to be surprised and challenged by new insights and perspectives, and trust in the unfolding of your own unique journey.

2. Seek clarification and support:

If you are unsure about a particular aspect of Gene Keys, don't hesitate to seek clarification and support from trusted teachers, mentors, or community members. The Gene Keys community is a rich resource of wisdom and experience, and there are many individuals who are committed to supporting others on the path of growth and transformation.

3. Trust your own inner knowing:

Ultimately, the most important guide on your journey with Gene Keys is your own inner knowing. While the teachings and practices of Gene Keys can offer valuable guidance and support, it's up to you to discern what resonates and what doesn't, and to trust in the wisdom and intelligence of your own being.

4. Embrace paradox and complexity:

The world of Gene Keys is one of paradox and complexity, where seemingly contradictory truths can coexist and inform one another. Rather than trying to resolve or eliminate these tensions, learn to hold them with grace and curiosity, and allow them to deepen and enrich your understanding of yourself and the world.

Summary

In this chapter, we've explored some of the common misunderstandings and misconceptions that can arise when working with Gene Keys, and provided guidance for navigating these challenges with clarity and understanding. By embracing curiosity, seeking support, trusting your own inner knowing, and holding paradox and complexity, you can deepen your engagement with the teachings and practices of Gene Keys, and unlock the full potential of your being.

As you continue on your journey with Gene Keys, remember that the path of transformation is not always easy or straightforward, but it is always worth it. With patience, persistence, and a deep commitment to your own growth and evolution, you can transform your life and contribute to the healing and awakening of the world.

In the next chapter, we'll explore some real-life case studies and examples of individuals who have used Gene Keys for personal transformation, and highlight the different paths and approaches that are possible on this journey of discovery and awakening.

Chapter 7: Case Studies and Examples

In the previous chapters, we've explored the theoretical foundations and practical applications of Gene Keys, and examined some of the common misunderstandings and challenges that can arise along the way. In this chapter, we'll bring these teachings to life by sharing real-world case studies and examples of individuals who have used Gene Keys for personal transformation and growth.

These stories highlight the diversity and richness of the Gene Keys journey, and illustrate the many different paths and approaches that are possible on this path of discovery and awakening. By exploring these examples, you can gain inspiration and insight for your own journey, and see how the teachings and practices of Gene Keys can be applied in practical and transformative ways.

Case Study 1: Sarah's Journey of Self-Discovery

Sarah, a 35-year-old marketing executive, first encountered Gene Keys during a time of deep personal crisis and uncertainty. She had recently gone through a painful divorce, and was struggling to find meaning and purpose in her life. When a friend introduced her to Gene Keys, Sarah was initially skeptical, but decided to explore the teachings with an open mind.

As Sarah began to work with her Hologenetic Profile, she was struck by the accuracy and depth of the insights it provided. She discovered that her Activation Sequence was centered around the 51st Gene Key, which is associated with the shadow of agitation and the gift of initiative. Sarah realized that much of her life had been driven by a restless sense of agitation and dissatisfaction, and that she had often struggled to find a sense of direction or purpose.

Through the practice of contemplation and meditation, Sarah began to cultivate the gift of initiative, and to channel her restless energy into more constructive and creative pursuits. She started a blog and began to share her experiences and insights with others, and found a new sense of meaning and fulfillment in her life.

As Sarah continued to work with her Gene Keys, she also began to explore her Venus Sequence, which revealed a deep-seated pattern of codependency and people-pleasing in her relationships. With the support of a therapist and a close circle of friends, Sarah began to confront and transform these patterns, and to cultivate more authentic and empowered ways of relating to others.

Today, Sarah is a successful coach and mentor, and uses her own journey of transformation to inspire and support others on their paths of growth and self-discovery. She credits Gene Keys with providing her with a powerful framework for understanding herself and navigating the challenges of life with greater wisdom and resilience.

Case Study 2: Michael's Path of Spiritual Awakening

Michael, a 28-year-old software engineer, had always been interested in spirituality and personal growth, but had struggled to find a path that resonated with him. He had explored various teachings and practices over the years, but often felt like he was simply skimming the surface of a deeper truth.

When Michael discovered Gene Keys, he was immediately drawn to the depth and complexity of the teachings, and felt a strong resonance with the idea of the journey from shadow to gift to siddhi. He began to work with his Hologenetic Profile, and was particularly struck by his Pearl Sequence, which revealed a deep-seated pattern of scarcity and lack in his relationship to abundance and prosperity.

Through the practice of contemplation and embodiment, Michael began to confront and transform these patterns, and to cultivate a greater sense of trust and flow in his life. He also began to explore his Activation Sequence, which was centered around the 43rd Gene Key, associated with the shadow of deafness and the gift of insight.

As Michael continued to work with his Gene Keys, he began to experience profound shifts in his consciousness and perception. He found himself accessing deeper states of meditation and contemplation, and experiencing moments of profound insight and revelation. He also began to feel a greater sense of connection and unity with all of life, and a deeper sense of purpose and meaning in his work and relationships.

Today, Michael is a teacher and guide in the Gene Keys community, and uses his own path of awakening to support and inspire others on their journeys of transformation. He sees Gene Keys as a powerful catalyst for spiritual evolution and enlightenment, and is committed to sharing the teachings with as many people as possible.

Case Study 3: Lisa's Journey of Embodiment

Lisa, a 42-year-old yoga teacher and mother of two, had always been interested in holistic health and wellness, but had often struggled to find a sense of balance and integration in her life. She was drawn to Gene Keys as a way of deepening her understanding of herself and her place in the world, and of finding greater harmony and flow in her daily life.

As Lisa began to work with her Hologenetic Profile, she was particularly struck by her Venus Sequence, which revealed a deep-seated pattern of self-doubt and insecurity in her relationships. Through the practice of embodiment and movement, Lisa began to confront and transform these patterns, and to cultivate a greater sense of self-love and self-acceptance.

She also began to explore her Pearl Sequence, which was centered around the 2nd Gene Key, associated with the shadow of dislocation and the gift of orientation. Lisa realized that much of her life had been characterized by a sense of dislocation and disconnection, and that she had often struggled to find her place and purpose in the world.

Through the practice of contemplation and meditation, Lisa began to cultivate the gift of orientation, and to find a deeper sense of grounding and belonging in her life. She also began to integrate the teachings of Gene Keys into her yoga classes and workshops, and to share the practices of embodiment and self-inquiry with her students and clients.

Today, Lisa is a respected teacher and guide in the holistic health community, and uses her own journey of transformation to inspire and support others on their paths of growth and self-discovery. She sees Gene Keys as a powerful tool for cultivating greater harmony and integration in all aspects of life, and is committed to sharing the teachings with as many people as possible.

Summary

These case studies and examples illustrate the diversity and richness of the Gene Keys journey, and highlight the many different paths and approaches that are possible on this path of discovery and awakening. Whether you are seeking greater self-understanding, spiritual growth, or embodied transformation, the teachings and practices of Gene Keys offer a powerful framework for navigating the challenges and opportunities of life with greater wisdom and resilience.

As you continue on your own journey with Gene Keys, remember that your path is unique and precious, and that there is no one "right" way to engage with the teachings. Trust in the wisdom and intelligence of your own being, and allow yourself to be guided by your own inner knowing and experience.

And remember, too, that you are not alone on this path. The Gene Keys community is a rich and diverse network of individuals who are committed to personal and collective transformation, and who are here to support and inspire you on your journey. By connecting with others and sharing your own experiences and insights, you can deepen your engagement with the teachings and practices of Gene Keys, and contribute to the healing and awakening of the world.

In the next chapter, we'll explore some additional resources and further reading for those who want to delve deeper into the world of Gene Keys, and continue their journey of discovery and transformation.

Chapter 8: Resources and Further Reading

As you continue on your journey with Gene Keys, you may find yourself eager to delve deeper into the teachings and practices, and to connect with others who share your passion and curiosity. In this final chapter, we'll provide a list of recommended resources and further reading to support you on your path of discovery and transformation.

Books by Richard Rudd

Richard Rudd is the founder of the Gene Keys teachings, and has written several books that explore the depths and nuances of this powerful system. If you're looking to deepen your understanding of Gene Keys, these books are an excellent place to start:

1. *The Gene Keys: Embracing Your Higher Purpose* (2013) - This is the foundational text of the Gene Keys teachings, and provides a comprehensive overview of the system, including the 64 Gene Keys, the three sequences, and the journey from shadow to gift to siddhi.

2. *The Art of Contemplation: A Gentle Path to Wholeness and Prosperity* (2015) - In this book, Richard Rudd explores the practice of contemplation as a powerful tool for personal and collective transformation, and offers practical guidance and inspiration for integrating this practice into daily life.

3. *The 64 Ways: An I Ching Journey into the Mystery of Existence* (2017) - This book is a poetic and profound exploration of the 64 hexagrams of the I Ching, which form the basis of the Gene Keys system. Each hexagram is associated with a specific Gene Key, and Rudd provides insights and reflections on the deeper meanings and implications of each.

Online Courses and Programs

In addition to his books, Richard Rudd has also created several online courses and programs that offer a more immersive and interactive experience of the Gene Keys teachings. These include:

1. The Golden Path - This is a comprehensive online program that guides participants through the three sequences of the Gene Keys, and provides a deep dive into the shadows, gifts, and siddhis of each Gene Key. The program includes video teachings, guided meditations, and interactive exercises, and is designed to support participants in integrating the teachings into their daily lives.

2. The Activation Sequence - This online course focuses specifically on the Activation Sequence of the Gene Keys, and provides a step-by-step guide to unlocking the full potential of this powerful tool for personal transformation. The course includes video teachings, guided contemplations, and practical exercises, and is designed to support participants in navigating the journey from shadow to gift to siddhi.

3. The Venus Sequence - This online course explores the Venus Sequence of the Gene Keys, which focuses on the path of love, relationships, and the feminine aspect of consciousness. The course includes video teachings, guided meditations, and interactive exercises, and is designed to support participants in cultivating more authentic and empowered ways of relating to themselves and others.

Online Communities and Forums

One of the greatest gifts of the Gene Keys teachings is the global community of individuals who are committed to personal and collective transformation. By connecting with others who share your passion and curiosity, you can deepen your engagement with the teachings, and find support and inspiration on your journey. Here are a few online communities and forums to explore:

1. The Gene Keys Network - This is the official online community of the Gene Keys teachings, and provides a platform for connecting with other Gene Keys enthusiasts from around the world. The network includes forums for discussion and sharing, as well as a directory of Gene Keys practitioners and events.

2. The Gene Keys Facebook Group - This is a vibrant and active community of Gene Keys enthusiasts on Facebook, with over 10,000 members from around the world. The group provides a space for sharing insights, asking questions, and connecting with others who are exploring the teachings.

3. The Gene Keys Subreddit - This is a smaller but growing community of Gene Keys enthusiasts on Reddit, with around 1,000 members. The subreddit provides a space for discussion and sharing, as well as links to relevant articles, videos, and resources.

Retreats and Live Events

Finally, if you're looking for a more immersive and embodied experience of the Gene Keys teachings, there are many retreats and live events offered around the world. These events provide an opportunity to dive deep into the teachings, connect with others in person, and experience the transformative power of the Gene Keys in a supportive and nurturing environment.

Some of the most popular Gene Keys events include:

1. The Gene Keys Journey - This is an annual seven-day retreat led by Richard Rudd, which provides a deep dive into the Gene Keys teachings and practices. The retreat is held in different locations around the world each year, and includes daily teachings, meditations, and experiential exercises.

2. The Gene Keys Ambassadors Retreat - This is an annual gathering of Gene Keys ambassadors and practitioners from around the world, who come together to deepen their engagement with the teachings and support one another on their paths of service and transformation.

3. Gene Keys Workshops and Seminars - There are many Gene Keys workshops and seminars offered around the world, led by certified Gene Keys teachers and practitioners. These events range from one-day introductory workshops to multi-day immersive retreats, and provide an opportunity to explore the teachings in a focused and supportive environment.

Conclusion

We hope that this list of resources and further reading has provided you with some valuable guidance and inspiration for continuing your journey with Gene Keys. Remember that the path of transformation is not always easy, but it is always worth it. Trust in the wisdom and intelligence of your own being, and allow yourself to be guided by your own inner knowing and experience.

As you explore these resources and connect with others in the Gene Keys community, remember to approach the teachings with an open heart and a curious mind. Allow yourself to be surprised and challenged by new insights and perspectives, and trust in the unfolding of your own unique journey.

And above all, remember that the ultimate goal of the Gene Keys teachings is not just personal transformation, but collective awakening and healing. By doing the deep work of confronting your own shadows and cultivating your gifts and siddhis, you are not only transforming yourself, but also contributing to the evolution of human consciousness and the creation of a more just, compassionate, and sustainable world.

So go forth with courage, compassion, and curiosity, and know that you are part of a global community of individuals who are committed to the same noble purpose. Together, we can unlock the full potential of our being, and create a world that truly reflects the beauty, wisdom, and love that lies at the heart of all things.

Appendices

Appendix A: Glossary of Gene Keys Terminology

- Activation Sequence: The sequence of Gene Keys that reflects your life path and the unique challenges and opportunities for transformation that you will encounter along the way.
- Codon: In genetics, a codon is a sequence of three DNA base pairs that corresponds to a specific amino acid or stop signal during protein synthesis. In the Gene Keys, each of the 64 codons corresponds to a specific Gene Key.
- Contemplation: A core practice in the Gene Keys teachings that involves deep reflection, meditation, and self-inquiry into the nature of your being and the world around you.
- Gene Key: A specific archetypal energy or teaching that corresponds to one of the 64 codons in human DNA. Each Gene Key has a shadow, gift, and siddhi frequency.
- Gift: The positive expression or potential of a Gene Key that emerges when you transform your shadows and unlock your true essence.
- Hologenetic Profile: A unique map of your individual Gene Keys based on your time and place of birth, which reflects your specific path of transformation and awakening.
- Pearl Sequence: The sequence of Gene Keys that reflects your prosperity and material abundance, and the specific challenges and opportunities you will encounter in this area of your life.
- Shadow: The negative or challenging expression of a Gene Key that arises from unresolved trauma, conditioning, or limiting beliefs.

- Siddhi: The highest expression or embodiment of a Gene Key that emerges when you fully integrate your shadows and gifts and awaken to your true nature.
- Spectrum of Consciousness: The range of frequencies or expressions of a Gene Key, from shadow to gift to siddhi, which reflects the journey of transformation and awakening.
- Venus Sequence: The sequence of Gene Keys that reflects your relationships and the specific challenges and opportunities you will encounter in your connections with others.

Appendix B: Worksheets and Reflection Questions

1. Exploring Your Hologenetic Profile

- What are the key themes and patterns that emerge in your Activation Sequence, Venus Sequence, and Pearl Sequence?
- What insights or revelations do you have about your specific path of transformation and awakening?
- What challenges or obstacles do you anticipate encountering along the way, and how might you navigate them with greater wisdom and compassion?

2. Contemplating Your Shadows and Gifts

- Choose a specific Gene Key from your Hologenetic Profile and reflect on its shadow and gift expressions.
- What experiences or patterns in your life reflect the shadow frequency of this Gene Key?

- What qualities or capacities do you need to cultivate in order to transform this shadow and unlock the gift frequency?
- What steps can you take to integrate this gift more fully into your life and relationships?

3. Envisioning Your Siddhis

- Choose a specific Gene Key from your Hologenetic Profile and reflect on its siddhi frequency.
- What would it feel like to fully embody this siddhi in your life and being?
- What qualities or capacities do you need to cultivate in order to awaken to this highest potential?
- What steps can you take to align your thoughts, words, and actions with this siddhi frequency?

4. Integrating the Teachings into Daily Life

- What specific practices or rituals can you incorporate into your daily life to deepen your engagement with the Gene Keys teachings?
- How can you bring greater presence, compassion, and curiosity to your interactions with others and the world around you?
- What resources or support do you need to sustain your journey of transformation and awakening over the long term?

Appendix C: Additional Resources and Recommendations

1. Books

- "The Wisdom Keepers: The 64 Faces of Awakening" by Richard Rudd
- "The Kabbalah of Light: Ancient Practices to Ignite Your Imagination and Illuminate Your Life" by Catherine Shainberg
- "The Essentials of Vedic Wisdom for Blissful Living" by David Frawley

2. Online Courses and Programs

- The Gene Keys Society Membership
- The Gene Keys Dare to Dream Program

3. Podcasts and Interviews

- The Gene Keys Podcast with Richard Rudd
- Interviews with Richard Rudd on Buddha at the Gas Pump, Conscious TV, and Beyond Belief
- The Gene Keys on the Science and Nonduality Podcast

4. Retreats and Live Events

- The Gene Keys Annual Global Summit

- The Gene Keys Breakthrough Retreat
- The Gene Keys Wisdom Keepers Retreat

Remember that these are just a few examples of the many resources and opportunities available to support you on your Gene Keys journey. Trust your own intuition and inner guidance as you explore what resonates most deeply with your unique path and purpose.

Disclaimer:

This ebook, "An Introduction to The Gene Keys: A Beginners Guide To Better Understanding Yourself," was generated by an AI language model, Claude, developed by Anthropic. The content, insights, and information presented in this ebook are based on the AI's pre-existing knowledge base, which was trained on a vast corpus of text data up until 2021.

It is important to note that the AI does not have personal experiences or opinions, and while it can provide information and insights on a wide range of topics, it cannot guarantee the complete accuracy of the information provided. The AI's responses are generated based on patterns and information learned during the training process, and not from specific sources consulted for this particular writing task.

Therefore, readers are encouraged to verify the information presented in this ebook with official Gene Keys resources and materials, especially when it comes to the specific details and terminology related to the Gene Keys system. The AI-generated content should be treated as a starting point for exploration and understanding, rather than as a definitive or authoritative source of information.

As with any AI-generated content, there may be instances where the information presented is inaccurate, incomplete, or outdated. The creators of this ebook and the AI language model used to generate its content cannot be held liable for any errors, omissions, or inaccuracies present in the text.

By reading this ebook, you acknowledge that the content was generated by an AI language model and that it should not be relied upon as a substitute for professional advice or guidance. Always consult official Gene Keys resources and materials, as well as qualified practitioners and experts, for the most accurate and up-to-date information related to the Gene Keys system and its application in your personal growth and transformation journey.

Jenna Parker

Printed in France by Amazon
Brétigny-sur-Orge, FR